YES SHE DID! *SHE* DID!

SPORTS

Yes She Did! Sports

Scobre Educational
2255 Calle Clara
La Jolla, CA 92037

Scobre Operations & Administration
42982 Osgood Road
Fremont, CA 94539

www.scobre.com
info@scobre.com

Scobre Educational publications may be purchased for
educational, business, or sales promotional use.

Cover and layout design by Jana Ramsay
Copyedited by Susan Sylvia
Some photos by Getty Images

ISBN: 978-161570-876-5 (Soft Cover)
ISBN: 978-1-61570-889-5 (Library Bound)

TABLE OF CONTENTS

CHAPTER 1
FRAGILE TO FEROCIOUS

When the U.S.A. Women's Track Team took the stage for the 4x100 relay in the 2012 Olympics, the nation held its breath. The starting gun exploded and the women raced around the track. When they crossed

VICTORY LAP

Allyson Felix, Bianca Knight, Carmelita Jeter, and Tianna Madison of Team U.S.A. celebrate their record-breaking victory in the 4x100m relay in the 2012 London Olympics.

the finish line, millions cheered. The U.S.A. had won gold and shattered a world record. As the United States sung its anthem, it was with pride for the amazing ladies who had represented the nation. However, there was a time when women were not allowed to compete. Less than 150 years ago, women were believed to be too fragile to even run!

When the first modern-day Summer Olympics were held in Greece in 1896, women were banned from the games. However, not all women agreed with the ban, including distance-runner Stamata Revithi. Revithi, a poor Greek woman, traveled to Athens in the hopes of making history along with the other runners. When she was not allowed to compete, she decided to protest by running the same marathon course the day after the men. She finished the course in five hours and thirty minutes. By the end, her shoes were so torn

they barely stayed on her feet. But she proved that women were just as capable as men in competition. Revithi's run, as well as the pro-tests of others, allowed women to compete in the next Summer Olympics.

Females quickly went from fragile to ferocious. They started up their own sports teams and joined competitive leagues. In 1920, advertisements began to put a new emphasis on athletic bodies and lifestyles. They used slogans such as "Grand-mother went bathing—girls

DID YOU KNOW...

In 1902 Madge Syers entered an all-male world championship figure skating competition and placed second. This caused officials to ban women from the championships until a women's division was created.

like Molly go in to swim." The new focus on the "athletic woman" showed girls that it was becoming "cool" to be an athlete.

The movement reached a peak when Title IX was passed in 1972. Title IX was passed to support women's equality by prohibiting gender discrimination in any educational arena. In other words, it made sure that women could not be excluded from sports based solely on their gender. It was also the bill that gave female athletics the funding that the movement needed to boom. All of the sudden, women received collegiate athletic scholarships, and schools invested money in jerseys and equipment for women.

FIGHT FOR EQUALITY

Prior to Title IX, women would never have considered wrestling as a high school sport.

However, this movement would not have been possible without the efforts of pioneer athletes paving the way. It has taken many courageous, determined women to force the change so that women everywhere, just like the U.S. women's track team, can have their chance to excel.

DONNING JERSEYS

Women went from fragile to ferocious as the popularity of the athletic movement increased.

CHAPTER 2
DREAM IN GOLD

Women did not instantly gain respect in the athletic world. It took talented, hard working women to spur the sports forward. These pioneer women, like Mildred "Babe" Zaharias, were able to break through the stereotypes and become successful in athletics.

Babe Zaharias was born in Texas in 1914. Growing up, Babe constantly competed with her brothers whenever she could. When she played on an elementary baseball team, she hit five home runs in a single game. It earned her the nickname "Babe" after Babe Ruth, legendary home run hitter of the major leagues. Growing up, she played every sport she could. When asked if there was anything she didn't play, she responded, "Yeah. Dolls."

Babe was playing sports at a time when female athletes were seen as "freakish." Most were not accepted, and they were even ignored by the media. That did not stop Babe. When she was a teenager, she told her parents that her life's ambition was "to be the greatest athlete who ever lived." And that's exactly what she strove to do.

Babe first excelled in basketball. When she was 15, she played for the Golden Cyclones, one of the best teams in the nation. She then turned her attention to track and field. Less than two years after she saw her first track meet, she qualified for the 1932 Olympics in four different events. During the Olympics she broke four world records and won two gold metals. However, Babe is most widely known for her golf career. She won countless tournaments, and is known as one of the greatest golfers, male or female, of all time.

Babe didn't care that everyone said she wasn't allowed to be an athlete because she was a girl. She did it anyway. Just by competing, she changed the way people looked at female athletes. The media went from teasing her, to calling her "the Greatest Woman Athlete of the Half Century." Babe proved that women could be feminine, as well as stud athletes.

SWING FOR SUCCESS

Babe Zaharias is still known as one of the greatest golfers of all time.

Babe wasn't the only woman making a difference in the athletic world. She was joined by Billie Jean King. Billie Jean King was arguably one of the greatest tennis players of all time. She won over 20 titles and competed all around the world. But she is most known for her single, most important match against Bobby Riggs.

In 1973, Billie Jean agreed to play a match against Wimbledon champion Bobby Riggs. It was the first time a woman had competed against a man, and both of them definitely felt the pressure. King, when asked about the match, said that "I thought it would set us back 50 years if I didn't win that match. It would ruin the women's tour and affect all women's self esteem."

So King did the only thing she knew how to do: she won. In the battle of the sexes, women came out resoundingly victorious. King beat Riggs by a landslide! The match was nationally televised and followed by people around the world. It was an important moment for women because it showed that not only can they be successful as "jocks," they can also compete on a

DID YOU KNOW...

Billie Jean King was the first woman athlete to win more than $100,000 dollars in a single season in any sport.

plane equal to men.

But that wasn't all Billie Jean did for women athletics. She also founded *womenSports* magazine and started a Women's Sports Foundation. Both on and off the court, Billie Jean helped people in the 1970s accept females as athletes. However, not all pioneers for athletics happened during the women's athletic movement. Some are still happening today!

ANOTHER ACE

Billie Jean King is the only woman to have won US singles titles on grass, clay, carpet, and hard courts.

Misty May and Kerri Walsh were not the first women to play beach volleyball, and they certainly won't be the last. However, they have been instrumental in taking women's beach volleyball into the national light and helping it become a sport women can be proud of playing.

Misty May-Treanor and Kerri Walsh-Jennings were both born into athletic families. Misty played in her first beach volleyball tournament when she was eight, and then continued to play indoor volleyball through college. After college, she decided to switch back to her childhood passion and get back on the beach. Kerri was raised on indoor volleyball, and became a dominant player at Stanford University, where she became the second NCAA player in history

RAISING STANDARDS

Kerri Walsh (left) has worked hard to make women's beach volleyball into a competitive league.

to be named First Team All-American all four years. After college, she didn't want to give up volleyball, yet she yearned for a change. After a conversation with Misty May, the duo decided to team up, and have been taking the beach by storm ever since.

Women established their own professional beach volleyball league in 1999. Though it was a major breakthrough for women, many critics still claimed that beach volleyball was a "man's sport" and women could never play as competitively. Kerri Walsh disagreed. She wanted to show the world how competitive women could be. So she did, with the help of her beach volleyball partner, Misty May.

May and Walsh's 13-year playing partnership ended in 2012 when they won their third straight Olympic gold medal—a feat never accomplished by any other duo in beach history. Misty May attributes this to her "dream in gold" attitude. She says that you should dream to be the best you can be. May and Walsh have been dreaming that they could be the best for a long time. It is why they have dominated the beach for over 12 years. Their success has helped bring not only them, but also women's beach volleyball, into the spotlight.

Both women agree that their success isn't only for themselves. It is for every girl who wants to play beach volleyball. They want to set a high standard to keep the level of play progressing. May said that "my best moments in life have been winning the three gold medals, and being able to share that with the world, with the young girls who are going to fill our places when we're done playing." Thanks to May and Walsh's success, there are lots of girls who are hoping to do just that.

Whether the athletic pioneers played years ago or only weeks, there have been many women who

TOP OF THE PODIUM

Misty May and Kerri Walsh had to beat the other U.S.A. women's team to win the gold in 2012. It was their third gold medal win in a row!

have made sports a popular and competitive pastime. However, in the midst of the pack, certain women stand out above the rest. Women like Missy Franklin and Abby Wambach are both rising above the ranks of their competitors.

CHAPTER 3
THE SPORT DOES THE TALKING

Missy Franklin, a 17-year-old from California, started swimming as a toddler. Her mom was terrified of water. She did not want Missy to grow up with the same fears, so she enrolled her in swim lessons. However, what began as a survival class quickly turned into Missy's favorite thing to do. When she easily won her first competition

GAINING GOLD

Missy Franklin won four gold medals and one bronze medal in her first Olympics at the age of 17.

in fifth grade, her parents knew that she was gifted.

Missy Franklin, nicknamed "Missy the Missile," has taken the pool by storm ever since. After numerous competitions and victories, Missy's career reached a new level in 2012 when she qualified for the London Olympics. She qualified for seven events, the most of any female swimmer in Olympic history. Many worried that it was too much for the young swimmer to handle. However, Missy did not share their concerns.

A FEMALE PHELPS

Missy gets her nickname "Female Phelps" from Michael Phelps. Michael Phelps won eight Olympic gold medals in the 2008 Beijing Olympics and has won 18 Olympic gold medals in his career. Here, Missy and Michael prepare for the London Olympics.

Despite her overwhelming swim schedule, Missy seemed to be constantly having a good time. Which is exactly what she was trying to do. Missy said that one of her goals was to smile at some point before every race: "I think it's important to take it all in and have that moment to look back on." Missy wanted to get more than a win out of her races. She also wanted to get a memory she could keep forever.

However, while Missy was all grins and giggles outside of the pool, when she jumped in the water she was all business. She was scheduled to race four individual events and three team relays, a schedule that earned her the nickname "Female Phelps," after Michael Phelps.

You would never know how crazy her schedule was when you watched her swim though. In each event she came out fast and finished faster, blowing

DID YOU KNOW...

As a kid, Missy was afraid of Santa Clause and E.T. Now other swimmers are afraid of her.

the competition away. At the end of her first Olympics, Missy finished with four gold medals and one bronze medal. And she was only a senior in high school.

In the face of the fame, Franklin remains humble about her accomplishments. When she competes, Franklin says a different side of her comes out: "It's okay to be humble outside of the pool, but be cocky when you're swimming." In the pool, her swimming speaks for her. And it says she's a champion.

Missy's not the only one whose sport says she's one of the best. By 2012, Abby Wambach established herself as

FORMIDABLE FORWARD

Abby (in blue) is known as a "forward," which means her main job is to score!

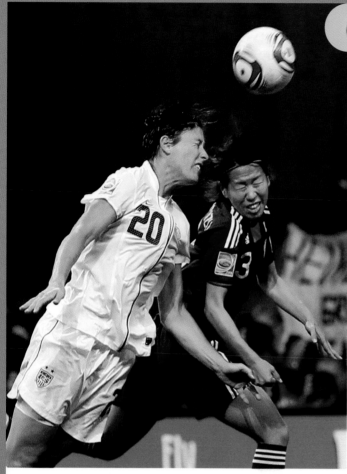

the most formidable offensive player on the national U.S.A. soccer team. Her talent has been inspiring, even at an early age.

When Abby joined her first soccer league at the age of four, it was evident that she had found her sport. After scoring 27 goals in the first three games, she was transferred from the girls' team to the boys'. Yet even that move did not stop her from dominating.

If anyone knows about Abby Wambach's career on the national level, it's her opponents. Any one of them can attest to her speed, determination, and ability to score under pressure. Especially the Olympic team from Brazil. They played the U.S.A. for the

Olympic gold medal in 2004. With only seconds left in overtime, Brazil and the United States were tied 2-2. Then the United States made their move. U.S.A forward, Megan Rapinoe, sent the ball into a melee of Brazil defenders, the Brazil goalie, and Abby Wambach. With the crowd holding its breath, Abby jumped above the defenders and the outstretched hands of the Brazilian goalie, and headed the ball straight into the net! Her goal put the U.S.A. up with less than a minute to play, and the U.S.A. won the gold medal.

Abby is known for her amazing scoring abilities. By the end of the 2012 Olympics, Wambach had scored 141 goals during her adult career. She was the second-highest scoring American, second only to Mia Hamm who scored 158. With much of her career yet to play, there's no doubt that she will soon take number one.

However, Abby is recognized and appreciated for more than just goals. Abby is a player with heart and determination. This was especially evident during her second trip to the Olympics. Though her goals were not the most flashy, they were scored at key times and they helped set the tone for the success of her team. Wambach scored in every single game in the London Olympics, with the exception of one. Her goals helped keep her team in the game, and give them the push they needed to succeed. Wambach has become known as the "American Hero" of the team, a reputation her play has lived up to. Yet her advice to young girls who look up to her is not to be like her. Abby tells them, "Don't try to be like Abby Wambach, be better than me."

DID YOU KNOW...

The youngest competitor on the 2012 U.S.A. Olympic team was Katie Ledecky, a 15 year old who won the 800m freestyle by over 4 seconds.

Abby Wambach and Missy Franklin are in vastly different sports, yet their stories are the same. Both

Abby, proudly holding an American flag, is known as the "American Hero" of the U.S.A.'s women's soccer team.

women are excelling above the competition. They continue to advance the level of skill in their fields. With women like Abby and Missy setting exceptionally high standards for women's athletics, the gap between male and female competitions is shrinking. And there are many women, like track Olympian Allyson Felix, who are striving to make it disappear completely.

CHAPTER 4
THE GAME CHANGER

DID YOU KNOW...

A sprint, long jump, triple jump, or hurdle will not be recognized as a new world record if the wind is too strong.

When Allyson Felix joined her middle school track team in the 7th grade, the other students nick-named her "Chicken Legs" for her lanky physique. However, despite her skinny legs, Allyson excelled right away as a sprinter. She went undefeated in middle school and high school state competitions. After high school, Allyson turned professional and her career exploded.

Allyson earned a spot on the U.S.A. track team for the 2004 Olympics at the age of 18. She was runner up in the 200 meter dash, just missing the gold behind Jamaican runner Veronica Campbell. In the 2008

Olympics, she was beat once again by Campbell.

Thanks to her fighting attitude, Allyson entered the 2012 Olympics with a vengeance. After four years of intense training, Allyson made history. She crossed the finish line ahead of all the other runners, including Campbell. Allyson's gold-medal finish began her dominating 2012 Olympic appearance. It led the way to two more gold medals and a new world record. By the end, she had earned the title of one of the fastest women of all time.

Allyson's success is mainly due to her training program. Unlike previous training programs for women, the United States women's track team follows a program almost identical to the men's. With the prejudices against women

STAR SPRINTER

Allyson has won more medals in the 200m dash than any woman in history.

athletes almost gone, the women's team is able to mix the athleticism of the men with the femininity of their gender. Allyson Felix can leg press 700 pounds, yet says "I love wearing heels. I wish I could wear them all the time, but, you know, my sport doesn't really permit it."

Allyson and the track team are not the only women proving that they can compete at the same level as male athletes. Women like tennis superstar Serena Williams are competing with the men, as well. Serena was raised on tennis, under her sports enthusiast father. From the age of three, Serena and her sister, Venus, practiced tennis for hours every day. And at the age of 12, it paid off. Serena turned pro-fessional, and by the age of 14, was ranked among

the top women tennis players in the world. When asked who she looked up to, Serena stated that "Billie Jean King is completely my idol." And like her idol, Serena didn't just want to be the best woman on the court—she wanted to be the best. Period.

At the age of 16, at the Australian Open, Serena and Venus boasted that they could beat any professional male tennis player ranked 200 or above. In response to their claim, Karsten Braasch, ranked 203, agreed to face each of the sisters. Despite their bold claims, both sisters fell easily to Braasch. When asked about the game, Serena said "I didn't know it would be that hard. I hit shots that would have been winners on the women's tour and he got them easily."

However, Serena was not discouraged by the loss. She proudly stated, "This time next year I'll beat him.

I have to pump some weight... I have to work hard to be on the men's tour." And that's exactly what she did. Though she never had her promised rematch against Braasch, Serena has been an inspiration in tennis, beating numerous male competitors while dominating in women's tournaments. Her loss to Braasch showed her what she had to do to succeed, and she has continued to do it throughout her career.

Brittney Griner, a basketball powerhouse, has also shown that she can do what any guy can do. Brittney, referred to by her coaches as "Miss All-Everything," didn't start playing basketball until her freshman year at Nimitz High School in Houston, Texas. However, the six-foot freshman quickly picked up the game. She first gained popularity at the age of 16, when a video of her displaying an array of dunks surfaced on YouTube. She was one of the only

DID YOU KNOW...

In the 1960s and 1970s it became typical for men to dunk so hard they shattered the backboard. All baskets now have shatter-resistant backboards and breakaway rims to avoid damage.

high school girls to ever dunk! Brittney set the record for the most dunks in a women's high school basketball game, dunking on Aldine High School seven times. Brittney continued to impress during her college career at Baylor College. By her senior year in 2012, Brittney stood six-feet, eight-inches tall, and led the NCAA in points, blocked shots, and dunks.

However, while most see Brittney's abilities as the potential standard for future women athletes to aspire to, some people are more negative. Critics claim that she is more male than female, and shouldn't be allowed to compete. But Brittney does not let their mean comments hurt her. When asked about the verbal abuse she receives, Griner replies that it doesn't

SLAM DUNK!

Brittney Griner is dunking her way into the record books!

Brittney must put up with critics every day, yet she continues to smile and play basketball, because she realizes that the only way to beat the critics is to keep excelling.

bother her because she knows it's not true: "I really don't care, they try to get in my head because they're trying to stop me. It's not going to work really. You'll see me smiling."

From training like men to actually competing on their level, women are slowly proving that they have the athleticism necessary to level the playing field of the sexes. Women like Allyson, Serena, and Brittney are positive examples of where the future of women's sports could lead. However, women are not only gaining athletic equality in the game. Many women are excelling in positions off the court as well.

CHAPTER 5
BEYOND THE COURT

For retired athletes and sports-enthusiasts, there are numerous careers to choose from. From coaching to refereeing to broadcasting, there are many women who have taken up supporting

GOING LIVE

While women were originally hired for looks alone, sports broadcasters, such as Bonnie Bernstein, must now be knowledgeable about the sport.

roles that make sports run smoothly and efficiently. One such woman is retired basketball sensation, Anne Donovan.

Anne Donovan was one of the most successful basketball players in the 1980s. As a six-foot, eight-inch center for Old Dominion University, she dominated the college scene, leading her team to a national championship and two more "Final Four" appearances. During her professional career, she won two Olympic gold medals. However, Anne is more known for her coaching ability than her playing career.

When Anne retired from the court, she took up a position as an assistant coach for

Old Dominion University. From there, she slowly made her way up the coaching ladder, eventually becoming a head coach in the Women's National Basketball Association. During her time in the WNBA, Anne became the first woman coach to take a team to the national championships. She's also the first female coach to win over 100 games. When asked how her accomplishment would alter the future of coaching for women, Anne responded, "The big picture is the more opportunities you have for women in this league, the more success we'll find for females." Anne proved that women can coach just as well as men.

Anne received the highest honor possible when she became the head coach of the 2008 U.S.A. Women's Olympic basketball team. While head coach, she led the team to a gold medal, despite the fact that the U.S.A.

team was not even expected to win. Through her accomplishments, Anne Donovan paved the way for women following her to succeed off the court as well. However, Anne is not the only basketball player who is known for her time off the court.

Violet Palmer, born in California in 1964, won two national championships when she played for California State Polytechnic University. When she retired from basketball, she chose a slightly different route than Anne Donovan: Violet Palmer decided to be a referee. She began by refereeing high school games in her free time. She was so successful though, that she was quickly promoted. In 1994, Palmer was asked to be a referee in the WNBA. Following her success there, she decided to go one step farther and become a referee in the men's professional basketball league. In 1997,

The Miami HEAT's LeBron James argues with Violet Palmer over a call during the game.

Violet Palmer became the first female to be a referee in the NBA.

    This was a huge step for women, yet many feared that Palmer would not be able to match the standards of the men. However, Palmer had no such fear. She knew that she was up to the challenge. Palmer has since proven herself as a capable referee, quieting the previous critics. Players and coaches no longer think of her any differently than any other referee. Lakers Coach Mike Brown, when questioned about her position in the league, said "It's not anything I think of, maybe because she's that good. She fits in and it seems natural for her to be an official for us." Like Palmer, there are other female referees, such as Shannon Eastin, who are proving that their gender does not alter their capabilities as referees in male sports.

Football, a sport thoroughly dominated by men, is not the usual place to find a female referee. However, Shannon Eastin had a passion for the sport. Since she couldn't play it, she decided to referee instead. Eastin, like Palmer, knew that she wanted to be a referee at the highest level. In 2012, she got her chance. In a preseason game between the Green Bay Packers and San Diego Chargers, Eastin became the first woman to referee an NFL game. In addition to making various calls as a line judge, Eastin also had to break up some players who were shoving each other after the game! However, Eastin never balked during any of her duties, proving that she was the right choice for the job.

Leading up to the game, both Eastin and the NFL made a point of downplaying Eastin's gender. As Eastin put it, "I hope to show it really doesn't

SMALL WONDER

Many people didn't want Eastin to be a referee in the NFL because they were worried that with her small size, she was likely to be hurt.

matter if you are male or female." She didn't want her debut game to be about her gender; she wanted it to

be about the quality of her refereeing. Which is exactly what it was.

Immediately after the game, Shannon was inducted into the Pro Football Hall of Fame in honor of being the first female referee in the league. Though she didn't want her job to be looked at from a gender bias, Eastin has nonetheless opened up the door of possibility for other female referees.

Eastin, as well as female athletes and competitors everywhere, have shown that the possibilities for women's involvement in sports are endless, if you're willing to work hard and strive for your dreams.